Presented to

_____

By

_____

On

_____

ZONDERKIDZ

The Rhyme Bible Storybook
Copyright © 1996 by L. J. Sattgast
Illustrations copyright © 2012 by Laurence Cleyet-Merle

Requests for information should be addressed to:

Zonderkidz, Grand Rapids, Michigan 49530

Library of Congress Cataloging-in-Publication Data

Sattgast, L. J., 1953–
    Rhyme Bible Storybook Bible / written by Linda Sattgast ; illustrated by Laurence Cleyet-Merle.
       p.   cm.
    ISBN 978-0-310-72602-9 (hardcover)
    1. Bible stories, English. 2. Christian poetry, American. 3. Children's poetry, American. I. Cleyet–Merle,
Laurence. II. Title.
    BS551.3.S285 2012
    220.9'505—dc23
                          2011021449

Editor: Barbara Herndon
Art direction & Design: Jody Langley

Printed in China

14 15 16 17 /DSC/ 8 7 6 5 4

The Rhyme Bible

STORYBOOK

Written by L.J. Sattgast

Illustrated by
Laurence Cleyet-Merle

ZONDERVAN.com/
AUTHORTRACKER
follow your favorite authors

Contents

A NEW WORLD

Genesis 1&2

The world was once
As dark as night,
But then God said,
"Let there be light!"
The light appeared;
It shone so bright!
And so began
The day and night.

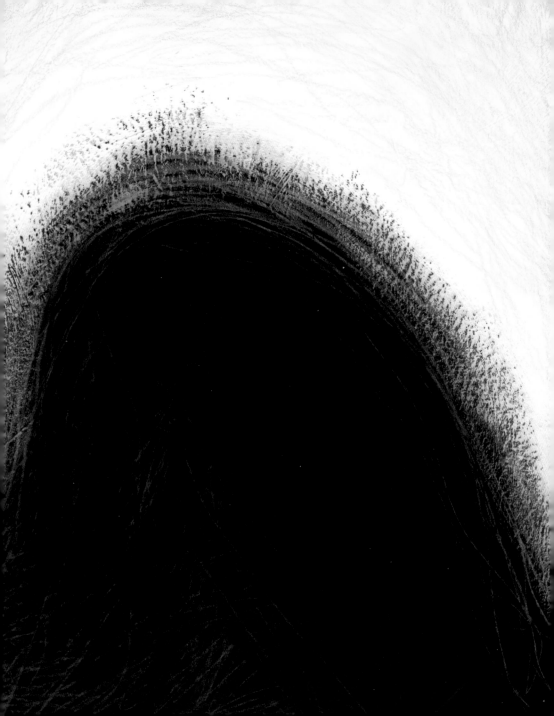

Then God made
The great big sky.
He made it wide;
He made it high,
With puffy clouds
To sail on by.
Oh, what a sky!

Then God made
The rocks and land.
He made the dirt;
He made the sand.
He told the plants
And trees to grow,
And it was so!

8

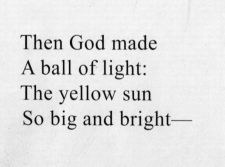

Then God made
A ball of light:
The yellow sun
So big and bright—

And moon and stars
To shine at night.
They were such
A pretty sight!

Then God spoke
These special words:
"Let there be
Some fish and birds.
Let them fill
The sea and sky
And swim and fly!"

12

Then God filled
The land with cats
And cows and sheep
And dogs and bats
And every creature
You can find—
God made each
And every kind.

14

15

Then God said,
"I have a plan.
I'll make a woman
And a man.
I'll let them rule
The land and sea.
They will be
A lot like me!"

And so it was,
When God was through,
And there was
Nothing left to do,
God decided
It was best
To have a special
Day of rest.

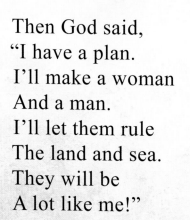

A SNAKE IN THE GARDEN
Genesis 3

God made a garden
So lovely and fair.
There were plants
And animals everywhere,
And Adam and Eve
Were happy there.

"You have all that you need,"
God told them one day,
"As long as you heed
The words that I say.
Here in the garden
There is a tree,
And the fruit on that tree
Looks as nice as can be.
But don't eat the fruit,
And I'll tell you why—
If you eat that fruit,
You will surely die!"

Adam and Eve
Were glad to obey.
They lived in the garden
Day after day.
But when the crafty snake
Came by, it spoke to Eve
And said, "Oh, my!
Did God *really* say
You had to obey?
I think you should
Try some anyway!"

Eve looked up
And saw the tree.
The fruit was as lovely
As it could be.
Should she pick some?
Should she eat?
Should she have
This special treat?
Or should she turn
Away her head
And just believe
What God had said?

The crafty snake
Was very sly.
He knew just how
To tell a lie.
"Eat the fruit
And you will see
How much like God
You'll come to be!"

Eve reached out
And took a bite.
Adam knew
It wasn't right,
But he ate some
Just the same.
Then he heard
God call his name.

God was sad
With Adam and Eve.
"You disobeyed,
So you must leave.
You can't come back
To your garden home,
But I will go with you
Wherever you roam."

SAFE IN THE BOAT

Genesis 6–9

God was very,
Very sad,
For all the people
Were so bad.
They would cheat,
And they would lie.
They would make
Their sisters cry.
They would kick
And steal and fight,
Though they knew
It wasn't right.
Noah was the
Only one
Who was pleasing
In God's sight.

God told Noah,
"Build a boat.
Make it strong
So it will float.
Make it tall
And make it wide,
And put a lot
Of rooms inside."

So Noah's family
Built the boat.
They made it strong
So it would float.
But all the people
Laughed and said,
"They are loony
In the head!

"Where's the water?
Where's the sea?
They're as crazy
As can be!"

God brought animals
Two by two.
They skipped and crawled
And hopped and flew
And squeaked and barked
And chirped and mooed.
The boat would be
A floating ZOO!

35

God commanded,
"Let it rain!"
And so it rained
On hill and plain.
Lightning flashed,
And thunder roared.
It sprinkled, showered,
Rained, and POURED!
The water got deep;
It covered the ground.
But those in the boat
Were safe and sound.

Days and weeks
And months went by
Before the ground
Was finally dry.
But then God said,
"It's time to come out!"
So out they came
With a roar and a shout!
And what did they see
When they looked up high?
A shining rainbow
In the sky!

ABRAHAM'S PRAYER
Genesis 15, 18, 21

Once upon
A moonless night,
When all the stars
Were shining bright,
An old, old man
Knelt down to pray,
And this is what
He had to say:
"How I long
To have a boy!
It would give me
So much joy!"

God was quick
With his reply,
"Go outside
And scan the sky.
Try to count
Each little star
That is twinkling
From afar.
If you can,
Then you will know
How big your family
Will grow!"

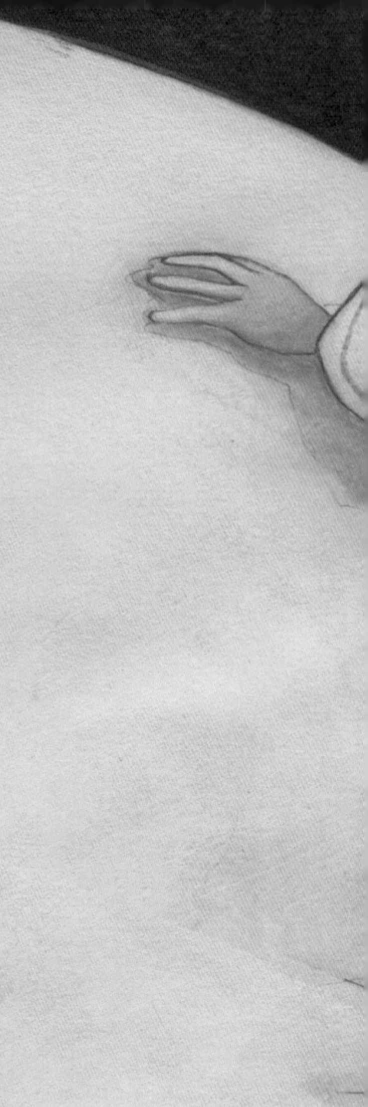

Many years
Went passing by,
And Abraham
Would often sigh
When he saw
The starry sky.
Yet each time
He climbed in bed,
He remembered
What God said.

Then one day
God sent some men
Just to tell him
Once again,
"God is sending
You a boy
Who will fill your
Heart with joy!"

Sarah laughed
Inside the tent.
"Is that *really*
What God meant?
I'm too old
To have a boy!
I will *never*
Have that joy!"

47

But God's promises
Are true.
What he says,
He's going to do.
So when nine more
Months were done,
Sarah had a
Baby son.
How they laughed
With pride and joy
As they held
Their little boy!

JOSEPH'S DREAMS

Genesis 37

Jacob had
A lot of sons,
But Joseph was
His favorite one.
"Look!" he said,
"Here's something new.
I've made a special
Coat for you!"
This made Joseph
Very glad,
But it made
His brothers mad!

Joseph had
A dream one night.
He dreamed the sun
Was shining bright,
And he was gathering
Some wheat
For his family
To eat.

All of a sudden
His sheaf of wheat
Stood straight and tall
In the summer heat.
His brothers' wheat
Came all around
And started bowing
To the ground.

53

54

Then Joseph dreamed
Another dream.
He wondered what
The dream could mean.
He saw the sun
And moon at night.
He saw eleven
Stars so bright.
They came and made
A ring of light
And bowed before him
In the night.

Joseph's brothers
Hated his dreams,
So all of them
Began to scheme.
They grabbed him
In the field one day
And took his precious
Coat away.

Then they sold him
To some men.
They thought they'd
Never see him again.

Down to Egypt
Went the men,
And Joseph had
To go with them.
They sold him to
the Pharaoh's guard
To be a slave
And work so hard.

THE KING'S DREAM
Genesis 39–41

Joseph slaved
And worked so hard
For Captain Potiphar,
the Pharaoh's guard.
But God was with him,
Potiphar could tell,
For Joseph's work
Turned out so well.

61

Now after quite
Some time went by,
Potiphar's wife
Told a great big lie.
"That slave you bought
Is up to no good.
He'd try to hurt me
If he could!"
So off to prison
Joseph went,
Although he knew
He was innocent.

Joseph wondered,
Does God care?
But even in prison,
God was there.
When two of the prisoners
Had some dreams,
Joseph said,
"Here's what they mean!"
God helped Joseph
On that day
To know exactly
What to say.

Then the Pharaoh
Had a dream.
It made him wonder,
What could it mean?
His servant said,
"I know of a man,
And *he* can tell you
If anyone can."
When Joseph came
Before the king
He said, "My God
Knows everything!
Tell me all about
Your dream,
And God will tell me
What it means."

"I dreamed," said the king,
"Of fourteen cows,
And though I cannot
Tell you how,
Seven fat cows
Were swallowed whole
By seven thin cows
Who were out of control.

"But the curious thing
About the matter
Was that none of the thin cows
Got any fatter!"

69

Then Joseph said,
"Here's what it means:
God is warning you
Through your dreams.
For seven years
We'll have good crops,
But after that
The rain will stop.
So find a man
To be in command,
And put him in charge
Of your majesty's land."

Pharaoh was glad
To hear this plan.
He quickly said,
"*You'll* be the man!"
He put Joseph in charge
Of everything,
And made him ruler
Next to the king!

JOSEPH AND HIS BROTHERS

Genesis 41–46

For seven good years,
While the land had rain,
Joseph collected
One fifth of the grain,
He put it in sacks
And stored it away,
For he knew they would need
To use it someday.

The good years ended;
The bad years came.
The fields became dusty
Without any rain.
The people cried out,
"There's nothing to hoe.
Please give us some grain—
Our crops won't grow!"

As soon as he heard
The people complain,
Joseph opened
The stores of grain.
Then one day
Some men came to town.
The men were his brothers,
And they all bowed down.
He looked like a king,
So how could they know
That he was the brother
They'd sold long ago?

Joseph spoke harshly.
He said, "You are spies!"
He did this to see
If his brothers would lie.
He wanted to know,
Would his brothers be good
And repent of their sins
And do what they should?

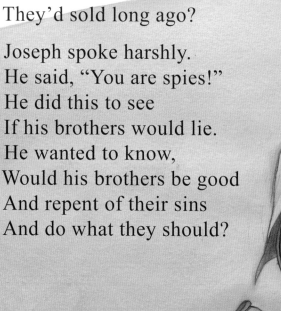

"We are not spies!"
The brothers said.
"We came here to buy
Some food and some bread."

Joseph gave them
Some food that day.
They loaded their sacks
And went on their way.
But Joseph had secretly
Opened one up
And put something inside—
His own silver cup!
Then, when the brothers
Had barely left town,
He sent some servants
To chase them all down.
They found the cup
In Benjamin's sack,
So they rounded them up
And brought them all back.

When the brothers saw Joseph
They tore their clothes.
They fell down before him
And said, "God knows
That we didn't steal
And we didn't lie,
But we're being punished,
And we think we know why—
We should have listened
When Joseph cried.
God saw our sin
Though we tried to hide!"

Finally, Joseph
Could stand it no more.
He sent out the servants
And closed every door.
Then he burst into tears
And said, "*I'm* the one!
I'm the brother you sold,
And it wasn't much fun!
But don't be afraid,
God planned it that way.
He knew I could help
My family someday."

Joseph's family
Lived far away,
But all of them traveled
To Egypt to stay.
When Jacob saw
His long, lost boy,
He hugged him and kissed him
And cried for joy!

83

THE PRINCESS AND THE BABY

Exodus 2

A long time ago
There lived a wicked king,
Who tried to do
A very wicked thing.
The king didn't like
The Israelites,
So he made a rule
That was very impolite:
"Throw the baby boys
Into the Nile!"
Said the evil king
With a wicked smile.

A certain mother
Had a baby boy.
He was cute and sweet,
And he brought her such joy!
"I *can't* throw my baby
Into the Nile,
So I'll try my best
To hide him for awhile."

But the baby made noise
Like all little boys.
So she took a little pitch
And she took some reeds,
And she made a basket-boat
That would suit her needs.
She went to the Nile
And let the basket float
While her daughter, Miriam,
Watched the little boat.

The Princess of Egypt
Came down the path.
She was coming to the river
To give herself a bath.
The Princess saw the basket
And was curious as could be,
So she said to her servants,
"Bring it here to me."

They opened the basket,
And the boy began to cry.
When he said, "Wahh! Waah!"
She began to sigh.
"It's an Israelite baby,
And he looks so sweet.
But I'm sure he's hungry
And would like to eat."

Then out came his sister
Who was hiding nearby.
She said she'd find a nurse
So the baby wouldn't cry.
The Princess agreed,
So she ran to find her mother.
How glad Miriam was
To help her baby brother!

He soon went to live
With the king's own daughter,
And she called him Moses
For she took him from the water.

OUT OF EGYPT

Exodus 2–15

Moses grew up
In the house of the king.
He lived in a palace
With every good thing.
But then one day
He made the king mad,
So he ran far away
And left what he had.

Moses tended sheep
Until a certain day
When he saw the burning bush
That didn't burn away.
He heard God speaking
In a voice loud and clear,
"Go down to Egypt and
Bring my people here!"

95

Moses went to Pharaoh,
And this is what he said,
"Let God's people go!"
But Pharaoh shook his head.
"They all belong to *me*,
And I *won't* let them go.
Besides, I will not listen
To a God I do not know!"

The Lord said to Moses,
"Listen to my plan:
When I'm through with Pharaoh
He will be a different man.
I'll fill the land with locusts,
And pesky frogs and flies,
But he still won't let them go,
For he isn't very wise.
So I'll send more plagues
Till the king agrees
That the Israelites can go
And do as they please."

Pharaoh wasn't happy
With all that God had planned.
At last he told the Israelites
That they could leave his land.
But just as they were leaving,
Pharaoh changed his mind.
He chased them with his soldiers,
Which wasn't very kind.

God said, "Listen,
You can trust in me!"
So he blazed a path
Through the waters of the sea.
When the soldiers tried to follow,
They fell into the sea.
Then the people all shouted,
"God has set us free!"

THE WALLS FALL DOWN
Joshua 1–6

The Israelites came
To the Promised Land.
A man named Joshua
Was in command.

The first thing they saw
In the valley below
Was a pretty little town
Called Jericho.

God told Joshua,
"There's something you
Should know.
It's all about the city
Called Jericho.
The people there are wicked,
So I'm giving you their town,
But you won't get in
Till the walls come down."

God told Joshua
Exactly what to do.
He told him to tell
All the people, too.
So early in the morning
At the break of day,
The people and Joshua
Started on their way.

First came some soldiers
Leading the way.
Then came the priests
With trumpets to play.
Next came the Ark of God
With priests all around.
And last came the rear guard,
But no one made a sound.

All around the city
The priests and soldiers walked.
But everyone was quiet;
No one even talked.
The trumpets gave a blast
The seventh time around.
Then the people all shouted,
And the walls fell DOWN!

SAMUEL LISTENS
Samuel 1–3

Hannah was sad
For she wanted a son,
So she went to the temple
To pray for one.
She promised God,
If he answered her prayer,
That her son would serve
In the temple there.

Nine months later
Hannah had a son.
She loved her son
More than anyone.
But while Hannah's son
Was still just a lad,
She took him to the temple
With all that he had.

The little boy, Samuel,
For that was his name,
Learned to help the people
Whenever they came.

Eli would show him
Exactly what to do,
And all the while
Little Samuel grew.

Then one night
When bedtime came,
He heard old Eli
Calling his name.
He ran to Eli,
But Eli said,
"I did not call.
Go back to bed!"

Then Samuel heard
The voice once more,
So he ran and knocked
On Eli's door.
But sleepy Eli
Shook his head,
"I did not call.
Go back to bed!"

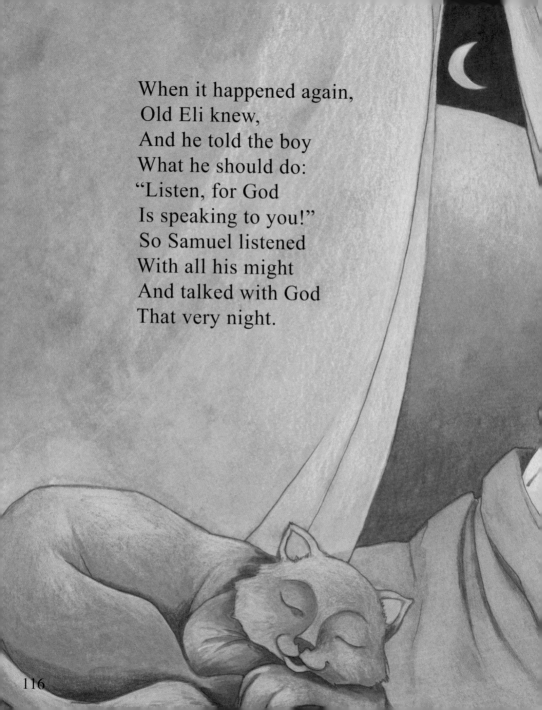

When it happened again,
Old Eli knew,
And he told the boy
What he should do:
"Listen, for God
Is speaking to you!"
So Samuel listened
With all his might
And talked with God
That very night.

DAVID & GOLIATH
1 Samuel 17

Who was mean
And tall and strong?
A giant named Goliath!
Who had a spear
That was sharp and long?
A giant named Goliath!

Every morning
And every night
Goliath tried
To pick a fight.
"Come and get me
If you can!"
But all God's people
Turned and ran.

119

A boy named David
Came one day.
He heard what Goliath
Had to say.
But David said,
"This man's a clod!
He's making fun
Of the living God!"

The king found out
What David said,
But then the king
Just shook his head.
"How can someone
As young as you
Expect to do what
A soldier can't do?"
"God will be with me,"
David said.
So at last the king
Nodded his head.

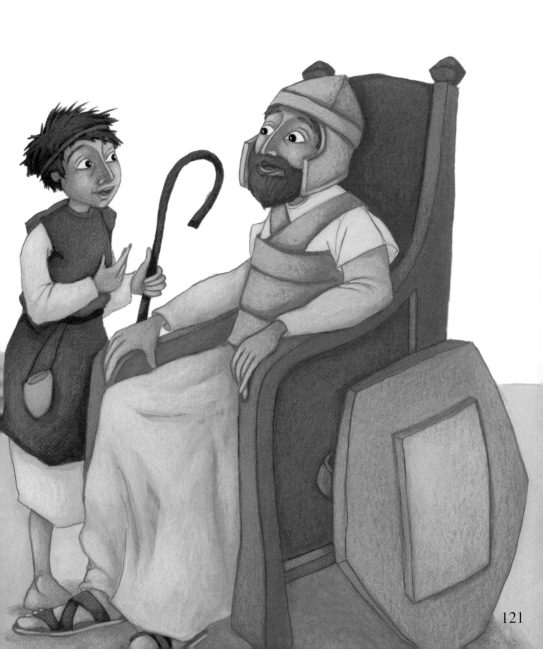

David turned
And left the king.
He took his staff
And he took his sling.
He walked on down
To a little stream
Where he found five stones
That were smooth and clean.

Goliath saw David,
And it made him mad.
He let out a roar
To frighten the lad.
But David kept coming.
He didn't run away.
And that's when Goliath
Heard him say,
"*You* come to me
With a spear and a sword.
But *I* come to you
In the name of the LORD!"
David made the sling
Go around and around.
The stone flew up
With a whistling sound,
And giant Goliath
Fell to the ground!

ELIJAH AND THE PROPHETS
1 Kings 16–18

Elijah, the prophet,
Went to see the king.
He went with a message
God wanted him to bring.
"There won't be any rain,
And there won't be any dew.
For you worship idols,
And your wife does too!"

God sent Elijah
To live by a brook.
There wasn't any food,
But he didn't have to look,
For God sent ravens
With some bread and meat.
So he drank from the brook
And he had enough to eat.

Three years passed,
And the land was very dry.
Elijah met the king
On a mountain nearby.
He said to the king,
"Now, here's what we'll do:
It's time to find out
Which god is true!"

The prophets of Baal
Danced all around.
They prayed to their god,
But he didn't make a sound.
Elijah joked,
"Could your god be asleep?"
So they shouted even louder,
But they didn't hear a peep.

Elijah stepped forward,
And after he had prayed,
Fire fell from heaven
To the altar he had made.
It burned up the altar,
The stones, and the sod,
So the people all shouted,
"The LORD—he is God!"

Elijah prayed for rain
With his face to the ground.
At first there were no clouds,
And he didn't hear a sound.
But then the sky grew black,
And the wind began to blow,
And down came the rain
To the thirsty land below!

JONAH GOES TO NINEVEH
Book of Jonah

God said to Jonah,
"I have a little task.
Get up and go to Nineveh
And do what I ask.

"The people there are wicked,
So tell them to obey."
But Jonah got on board a ship
And sailed the other way!
(Uh-oh, Jonah,
You better go to Nineveh!)

God sent a windstorm
To shake up the boat.
The frightened sailors worried
That it wouldn't stay afloat.
Jonah had been sleeping,
But he heard the captain cry,
"Everybody pray—
Or we all may die!"
(Uh-oh, Jonah,
You should've gone
To Nineveh!)

Jonah told the sailors,
"It's all because of me.
I'm sure the wind will stop
If you throw me in the sea."
They didn't want to do it,
But the wind howled and roared.
So they picked up Jonah
And threw him overboard!
(Uh-oh, Jonah,
You should've gone to Nineveh!)

When Jonah hit the water,
The wind stopped blowing.
The boat stopped lurching,
And the waves stopped rolling.

But God prepared a fish,
And as soon as it arrived,
It opened up its mouth
And swallowed him alive!

(Uh-oh, Jonah,
You should've gone
To Nineveh!)

Down went Jonah
With a great big SWISH!
He landed at the bottom
In the belly of the fish.
For three days and three nights
He stayed that way.
Then he prayed for help,
And promised to obey!

(That's better, Jonah,
It's time to go to Nineveh!)

Jonah was relieved
When he saw what God had planned.
The fish threw him up
And tossed him on the land.
God said to Jonah,
"I want them to repent,
So go preach to Nineveh."
And this time Jonah went!

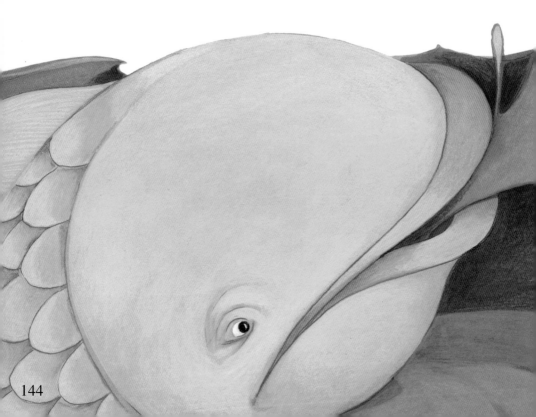

(That's good, Jonah!
I'm glad you went to
Nineveh!)

145

DANIEL AND THE LIONS
Daniel 6

Daniel lived in Israel
A long, long time ago.
But when he was a lad,
He was captured by his foe.
They took him off to Babylon
And made him serve the king,
But Daniel prayed and lived for God
In spite of everything.

The king looked around
For someone wise and good,
Someone he could trust
To do the things he should.
The king picked Daniel,
But it made the others mad,
So they figured out a plan
To make Daniel look bad.

The men came before the king
And said, "You are so great!
May we suggest a simple rule
That you can legislate?
For thirty days and thirty nights
To you alone we'll pray.
The lions' den will be the fate
Of all who disobey!"

The king agreed,
And so the rule
Was made into a law.
The other men watched Daniel,
And this is what they saw:

Daniel went into his room
And, kneeling down to pray,
He thanked the Lord
And asked for help
Like every other day.

The men ran to tell the king
That Daniel disobeyed.
The king was sad, but couldn't change
The rule that he had made.
And so the men took Daniel
And brought him to the den.
They threw him to the lions.
Oh, what would he do then?

The king was so unhappy.
He couldn't sleep that night.
When morning came, he quickly ran
And cried, "Are you all right?"
Daniel answered, "Yes, oh king!
They didn't get a bite!
For God sent his angel
To shut their mouths up tight!"

ESTHER SAVES THE DAY
Book of Esther

Once there was a king
Who had almost everything.
But he still wasn't happy,
For he didn't have a queen.
The wise men suggested
That he issue this command:
Let a search be made
In every corner of the land!

Now Esther was an orphan
Who lived with Mordecai.
The king's men saw her
As they were riding by.
They took her to the palace
And brought her to the king.
The king was very
Pleased with her
And chose her as his queen.

Mordecai would often sit
Beside the palace gate.
He saw a man named Haman
Who was riding proud and straight.
When Haman looked at Mordecai,
His heart was filled with hate,
For Mordecai would never bow
As Haman passed the gate.
Haman was so angry
That he went and got permission
To kill God's special people,
The Jewish population.

The rule went out
Across the land
To people everywhere.
When Mordecai heard of it,
It filled him with despair.
He told Queen Esther,
"You must go
And kneel before the king.
Perhaps you can persuade him
To stop this awful thing!"

157

So Esther fixed a banquet
As soon as she was able.
She asked the king and Haman
To join her at the table.
The king was very happy
With the dinner she had made.
"Please tell me what you want," he said.
"You needn't be afraid!"

Esther cried, "Please spare my life
And save my people too!
This wicked man has made a plan
To murder every Jew!"
The king jumped up and hollered,
"Haman, is this true?

"Then you will die, and Mordecai
Will rule instead of you!"
The people made a holiday
To celebrate the way
That Esther saved her people's lives
On that important day!

NEHEMIAH BUILDS THE WALL
Book of Nehemiah

When Nehemiah served the king,
His face was always glad.
But one day when he came to serve,
His face was very sad.

The king and queen asked him why
And listened to his sad reply:
"Jerusalem is broken down,
And that's what makes me cry!"

The king let Nehemiah go
To help rebuild the city.
But when he saw Jerusalem,
His heart was filled with pity.
Its mighty walls
Were broken down
With rocks and rubble
All around.

"Come on! Let's build!"
He cried to all
The people in the town.

The people gladly went to work.
They got up with the sun.
And many stars were shining bright
Before the day was done.
The gates were first to be installed,
And then they started on the wall.
"Come on! Be strong!" Nehemiah said,
"We'll build it straight and tall!"

167

But there were some
Who said, "You can't!"
They laughed and then
Began to chant:
"Don't be a sissy!
Don't be a fool!
Stop your work,
And drop your tool!
Why do you build
Such a rickety wall?
Even a fox
Could make it fall!
Nah, Nah, na-Nah, Nah!"

The people kept on working,
But it gave them quite a fright
To hear that men were coming
Who would try to pick a fight.
From that day on they carried swords
While stacking stones or cutting boards.

"Never fear!" Nehemiah said,
"Our trust is in the Lord!"

When, at last, the work was done,
They gathered in Jerusalem
And listened while the Word of God
Was read out loud to them.
"Amen! Amen!" the people said.
They worshiped God and bowed their heads.
And then they went to celebrate
With special food and bread!

171

THE SPECIAL BABY

Luke 2

Clip, Clop.
Clip, Clop.
One little donkey,
So fuzzy and brown,
Is on his way
To Bethlehem town.
Clip, Clop.
Clip, Clop.

Mary will ride,
And Joseph will walk.
Both of them
Are too tired to talk,
For the road is long
And they cannot stop.
Clip, Clop.
Clip, Clop.

The fuzzy brown donkey
Perked up his ear
When Joseph cried,
"At last, we are here!"
But, oh, what a crowd—
So noisy and loud!
And where would they stay
At the end of the day?

175

"Do you have room?"
Poor Joseph said.
"We've come so far,
And we need a bed."
But the busy innkeeper
Shook his head.

Mary and Joseph
Turned away.
But then they heard
The innkeeper say,
"If you don't mind
Some cows and sheep,
I have a place
Where you can sleep."

The fuzzy brown donkey
Was glad to stay
Beside a manger
Filled with hay.
"Moo!" said a cow.
"Ba-a-a-a!" said the sheep.
Then everyone tried
To get some sleep.

178

And when the animals
Opened their eyes,
There in the manger,
To their surprise . . .

A baby lay!

It was Baby Jesus
Asleep on the hay,
A gift from God
On Christmas day!

THE SHEPHERDS
Luke 2

Late one night,
One quiet night,
Some shepherds sat
By the flickering light
When all of a sudden . . .

They saw something BRIGHT!
"What is it?" they cried
As they tried to hide,
For it gave them such
A terrible fright!

But then they heard
An angel say,
"Don't be afraid,
For on this day
A baby was born
On a bed of hay.
And even though
He is so small,
This baby is
The King of all!"

The shepherds heard
A wonderful sound—
Angels were singing
All around:
"Glory to God!"
They sang, and then,
"Peace on earth,
 Good will to men!"

The angels suddenly
Went away,
And with them went
The light of day.
Once again
The night was still,
And moonlight shone
On every hill.
The shepherds quickly
Ran with joy
To find this very
Special boy!

At last they found
Where the baby lay—
Fast asleep
Upon the hay!

189

THE WISE MEN

Matthew 2

Far away,
One cold, dark night,
Some wise men saw
A strange new light.
They looked at the sky
And wondered why
One star should be
So big and bright.

Then one of them said,
"The star must mean
That something GREAT
Is happening!
A special King
Was born tonight,
And that's the reason
For this light!"

Then all of them cried,
"Let's follow the star!
It may be near,
Or it may be far.
We'll search until
We find the place
Where we can see
The baby's face!"

So off they went
To follow the star.
And was it near?
Or was it far?
Oh, it was far,
So far away!
But on they traveled,
Day after day.

And then one night
The star shone down
Upon a house
In Bethlehem town.
And there they saw,
To their delight,
The reason for
The shining light.

The wise men's hearts
Were filled with joy
As they bowed down
Before the boy!
They gave their treasures
To the King
And went back home,
Still worshiping.

A LOST BOY

Luke 2

It was Passover time
In the spring of the year
As Mary and Joseph
Packed up their gear.
Jesus was glad
As the time drew near,
For Passover came
Only once a year.
His friends and relatives
Traveled with them
On the long, long road
To Jerusalem!

The city streets
Were crowded and hot
With merchants calling
From every spot.
There was so much to see
And so much to do
Before the holiday
Would be through.
But Jesus liked
The Temple best.
He loved to listen
And talk and rest.

201

When all the people
Got ready to go,
Mary and Joseph
Didn't know
That Jesus was not
Where they thought he would be—
With all of their friends
And their family.
So they walked for a day,
Then they looked all around,
But their twelve-year-old son
Was not to be found.

So back they both went.
They asked here and there.
They searched high and low,
They looked everywhere.
And after three days
Of hunting had passed,
They went to the Temple
And found him at last!

He was talking to teachers,
Discussing God's Word,
And the teachers could hardly
Believe what they heard.
"This boy is so young,"
They said with a nod.
"Yet see how he knows
So much about God!"

So Jesus went home
With his parents that day
And grew stronger and wiser
In every way.

JESUS IS GOD'S SON
Matthew 3–4

Down to the river
The people came.
It wasn't a picnic.
It wasn't a game.
The people came
To confess their sin.
Then John the Baptist
Said, "Come on in!
This is a way to
Show you repent."
So into the water
The people went.

A man walked up
To the riverside
And stepped into
The flowing tide.
John the Baptist
Was quite surprised
When he looked and saw
Those gentle eyes.

"Jesus!" he cried,
"Why did *you* come?
You've never sinned
Against anyone!"
But Jesus replied,
"God's will be done."

So Jesus was baptized
That very day
To show everyone
He would follow God's way.
Then a voice that came
From heaven above
Said, "This is my Son,
The One whom I love!"
And the Spirit of God
Came down like a dove.

That was when Jesus
Began to preach.
The people loved
To hear him teach!
They gathered around
In every town
And listened until
The sun went down.

Jesus welcomed
All who came.
He healed the sick,
The blind, the lame.
The things he did
Showed everyone
That Jesus really
Was God's Son!

FOUR GOOD FRIENDS
Mark 2

One poor man
Just sat and sat.
He sat all day
Upon his mat.
He couldn't walk.
He couldn't crawl.
He could not move
Around at all.

But four of his friends
Had come to say,
"We have good news
For you today!
We just found out
That Jesus came,
And he can heal
The sick and lame!"

The place where Jesus
Preached and taught
Was in a very
Crowded spot.
"There's no room,"
The four men cried.
"We will never
Get inside!"

Then the sick man
Heard them say,
"We will find
Another way!"
So they hunted
For a spot,
And they found it . . .

Way on top!

Through the roof
They dug a place
Right in front
Of Jesus' face.
"Never fear!"
The four men said,
As they lowered
Down the bed.

Jesus saw what
They had done.
And because
He was God's Son,
He was glad
To heal their friend
So that he could
Walk again!

THE STORM

Mark 4

Jesus was tired
From preaching all day.
"It's time," he said,
"To get away."
Near the dock
Some fishing boats lay,
So they got in a boat
And sailed away.

A gentle breeze
Began to blow
As the evening sun
Was sinking low.
The disciples sailed
Across the deep,
And Jesus soon
Fell fast asleep.

But suddenly
The wind grew strong.
It pushed the
Little boat along.
When thunderclouds
Began to form,
The disciples knew
It was a storm!

The waves grew tall
And splashed around.
The wind made such
A howling sound!
The little boat
Pitched up and down
Until they cried,
"We're going to drown!
Jesus, wake up!
Don't you care
That waves are
Splashing everywhere?"

233

Jesus lifted
Up his head.
He looked around
And then he said,
"Be calm! Be still,
O wind and sea!"
And it was calm
Immediately!

The disciples couldn't
Believe their eyes!
The storm had stopped,
To their surprise!
But Jesus said,
"You need not fear!
Didn't you know
That I was here?
Have faith in God—
He's always near!"

A SICK GIRL

Mark 5

A twelve-year-old girl
Lay sick in her bed.
Her father who loved her
Was worried and said,
"I hear that Jesus
Is teaching nearby.
Perhaps if I find him,
He won't let her die!"

The father went looking
And cried as he ran,
"I've got to find Jesus
As fast as I can!"
He ran through the village
And down every street.
He asked, "Have you seen him?"
To all he would meet.

At last, when he found him,
He fell on his knees.
"You've got to come with me!
Oh, please, Jesus, please!"
"Of course I'll come with you,"
Jesus replied.
So Jesus went with him
And walked by his side.

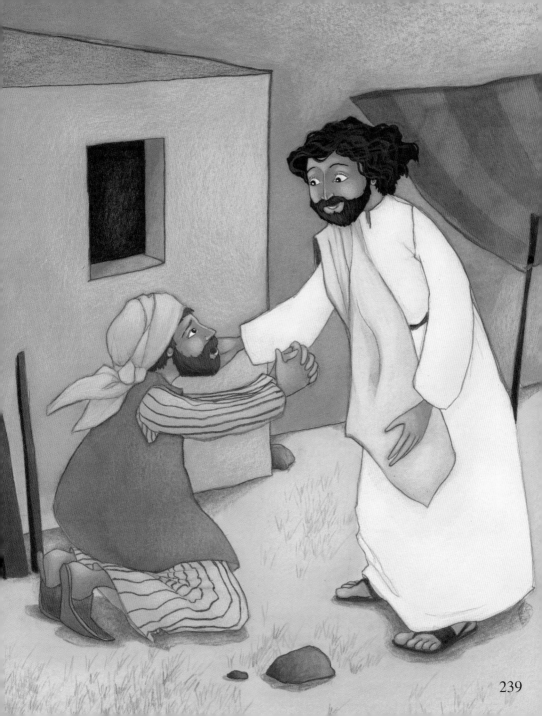

But just then a servant
Came running and said,
"Don't bother the Master.
Your daughter is dead!"
"Don't be afraid,"
Was Jesus' reply.

"Only believe,
There's no need to cry!"

241

Back at the house
The daughter lay dead.
But Jesus reached out,
And here's what he said,
"Get up, little girl!"
Then, what a surprise . . .

The little girl stood
And opened her eyes!

They never forgot
What Jesus had done,
For that's when they knew
That he was God's Son!

LUNCH TO SHARE
John 6

A boy once asked permission
To go hear Jesus talk.
"I'm sure it won't be far," he said,
"And I'll be glad to walk."
His mom agreed, but then she said,
"You'd better take a lunch,
For when a boy gets hungry,
He needs some food to munch!"

245

Into a basket went five loaves
And next to them two fish.
It was as nice a little lunch
As any boy could wish.
"Good-bye!" he said
And scampered off
To join the happy throng.
His mother waved
And called to him,
"Now don't be gone too long!"

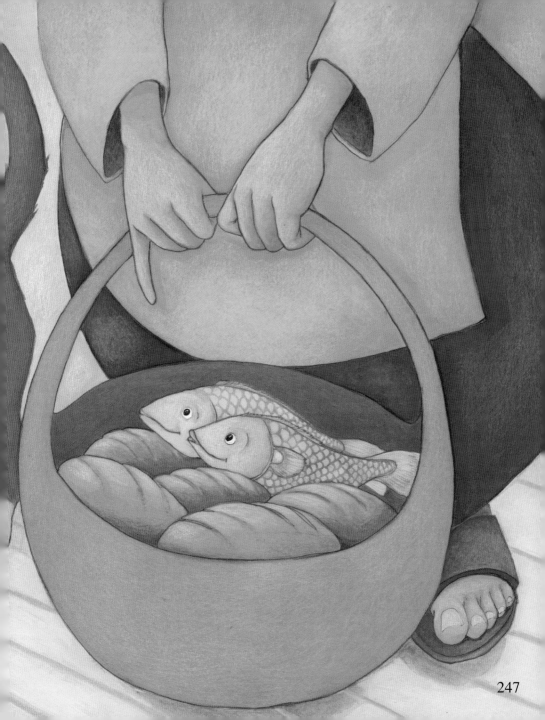

The little boy saw many things
Too wonderful to tell.
He saw how Jesus healed the lame
And made the sick ones well.

249

But when the sun
Was sinking low,
He heard kind Jesus say,
"Go and feed
This hungry crowd.
And don't send them away!"
But Philip said,
"It can't be done!
This crowd's too large to feed.
We'd have to have
A lot of cash
To buy the bread we need!"

And that is when the little boy
Tugged at Andrew's hand
And pointed to the basket
That was sitting in the sand.
"If you please, it isn't much,
But I will gladly share."
So Andrew went to Jesus
And set the basket there.

Jesus took the little lunch
And told the crowd to sit.
Then after he had given thanks,
He broke it into bits.

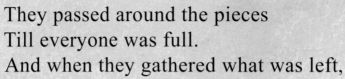

They passed around the pieces
Till everyone was full.
And when they gathered what was left,
They had twelve basketsful!

TWO HOUSES
Matthew 7

A wise man looked
Until he found
A firm and solid
Piece of ground.
On that rock
So strong and hard
He built a sturdy
House and yard.

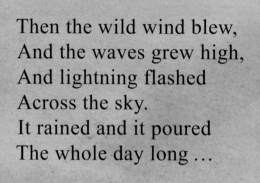

Then the wild wind blew,
And the waves grew high,
And lightning flashed
Across the sky.
It rained and it poured
The whole day long …

But the house on the rock
Stood firm and strong.

A foolish man found
A dandy place
With a lovely view
And a lot of space.
He built his house
On the shifting sand
And was quickly done
With his house and land.

Then the wild wind blew,
And the waves grew high,
And lightning flashed
Across the sky.
It rained and it poured
The livelong day . . .

And the house on the sand
Was washed away.

"So don't be like
The foolish man
And build your life
On shifting sand.
Listen and do
The things I say,
And you'll grow wiser
Every day!"

THE GOOD MAN
Luke 10

Jesus told this story one day:

There once was a man
Who was on his way
To visit a town
That was far away.

But out of the bushes
Jumped some thieves.
They didn't say thank you.
They didn't say please.
They took his things
And knocked him down
And left him bleeding
On the ground.

Not long after,
A priest came by.
He saw the man
And heard him cry.

Did the priest help?
Did he even try?

No, he did not.
He walked on by.

Next came a Levite.
He saw the man too.
And he thought to himself,

"What shall I do?
I'd rather not bother
With *that* kind of guy."
So he stepped to one side
And walked on by.

At last a Samaritan
Came that way.
He saw the man
And decided to stay.
He bandaged his wounds
And gave him a ride.
He fed him some food
And stayed by his side.

And when the Samaritan
Went on his way,
He counted his coins
And paid for their stay.

Then Jesus asked,
"Who did the good deed?

"Now go do the same
For someone in need!"

THE POOR RICH MAN
Luke 12

Once there was
A wealthy man
Who had a very
Stingy plan.
He put his money
On a shelf
And vowed to keep it
For himself.

He filled his bulging
Barns with wheat,
And though he had
Enough to eat,
He wouldn't share—
He didn't care
That others had
No bread or meat.

At breakfast time,
with toast and tea,
He liked to sing
This melody:

"I'm rich! I'm rich!
I'm filthy rich!
I'll never have
To dig a ditch
Or slave away
And work all day.
I'm rich! I'm rich! I'm rich!"

And when he ate
His lunch at noon,
He hummed a cheery
Little tune:

"It's nice to be
(Ho! Ho! Hee! Hee!)
A man as filthy rich as me!"

281

Although he filled up
Every drawer,
It only made him
Wish for more.
"I have three cats,
But I want four!
I have some cows,
But I want MORE!"

282

And when at last
He had no room,
This man began
To fuss and fume
Until he thought,
"Aha! Why not?
I'll build a bigger,
BETTER place
Where I will have
A lot of space!"

But there was something
He forgot.

285

Those who GET,
But never GIVE,
Choose a foolish
Way to live.
When that night
The rich man died,
Not one person
Even cried.

And what became
Of all his stuff?
Those who didn't
Have enough
Stood in line
That very day
As they gave it
All away!

A BOY COMES HOME
Luke 15

A young boy came
To his father one day
And said to his dad,
"I'm going away.
Give me the money
That's rightfully mine.

"I know how to spend it,
I'm sure I'll do fine."

291

The son took the money
And went on his way.
He was full of ideas
For fun and for play.
Oh, the things he would do
And the people he'd meet!
A life with no worries
Just couldn't be beat!
All of these thoughts
So filled up his mind
That he hardly remembered
The dad left behind.

At first he did well,
For he knew how to spend.
He would party at night
With all of his friends.
He never would work,
For he slept all day long.

He lived for excitement
And parties and song!

295

When his money ran out
One cold, rainy day,
He went to his friends
But they turned him away.
At last he found work
Feeding some swine.
He said, "How I miss
That father of mine!
My father's servants
Have plenty to eat
While I'm sitting here
With no bread and no meat.
I'll go to my father,
I'll try to be strong.
I'll beg for forgiveness.
I'll say 'I was wrong.' "

But while he was still
A long ways out,
His father saw him
And ran with a shout.
He hugged him and kissed him;
His heart filled with joy
As he welcomed back
His long lost boy!

299

CHILDREN COME TO JESUS
Mark 10

Some boys and girls
Went out to play,
But then they saw Jesus
Coming their way.

"Let's go see him!"
The children said.
And all the mothers
Nodded their heads.

301

But Jesus' disciples
Said with a frown,
"Just look at the children
In this town!
We can't allow
Those girls and boys—
They'll make entirely
Too much noise!"

So when the children
Came and said,
"We'd like to see Jesus!"
They shook their heads.
"Can't you see
He's busy teaching?
Don't interrupt
While Jesus is preaching!"

303

The children sadly
Turned away,
But Jesus called
For them to stay.
He scolded the men,
"Now let them be!
I want the children
To come to me!"

The children crowded
All around
And sat beside him
On the ground.
They laughed and had
A lot of fun
As Jesus blessed them,
One by one.

LITTLE ZACCHAEUS
Luke 19

There once was a man
Who never grew tall,
And hardly anyone
Liked him at all.
When people would see him,
They wanted to hide,
For little Zacchaeus
Cheated and lied.

It happened one day
That he heard someone say,
"I think I see Jesus
Coming this way!"
Zacchaeus hurried
And ran down the street,
For Jesus was someone
He wanted to meet.

But when he arrived
He groaned as he said,
"I'll never see over
All of these heads!"
And then, in a flash,
He knew what to do.
He knew where to find
A wonderful view!

Little Zacchaeus
Climbed up a tree.
"Hooray!" he shouted.
"Now I can see!"

Jesus came by
And looked in the tree.
"Zacchaeus," he said,
"Come eat with me!"
Zacchaeus was happy
To hurry on down
And walk with Jesus
Into the town!

Jesus soon left
And went on his way,
But little Zacchaeus
Was changed that day.
All of the people
Were happy to see
That he wasn't the same
As he used to be!

THE DAY JESUS DIED
John 18, 19

One day Jesus
Came to town,
And people threw
Their garments down.
They all began
To shout and cheer,
"Hosanna! Hosanna!
Jesus is here!"

But when the leaders
In that town
Heard the cheers,
It made them frown.
They didn't like
To see this man,
And so they made
A wicked plan.

They came to get him
Late at night
With all their torches
Burning bright.

The leaders took him
To a place
Where soldiers laughed
And hit his face.

321

And when the sun
Had risen high,
They put him on
A cross to die.
They didn't know
He was God's Son,
And that he died
For everyone.

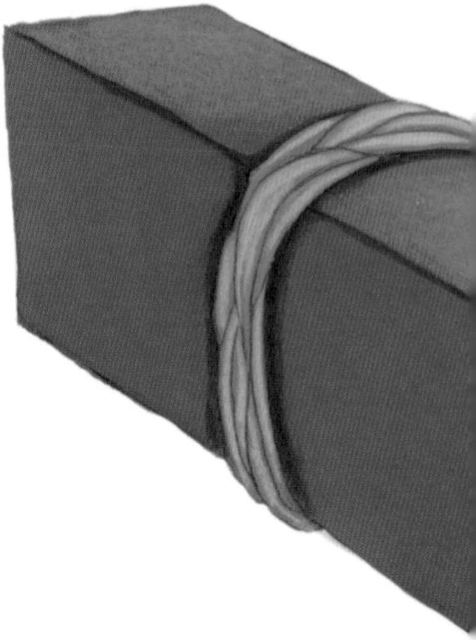

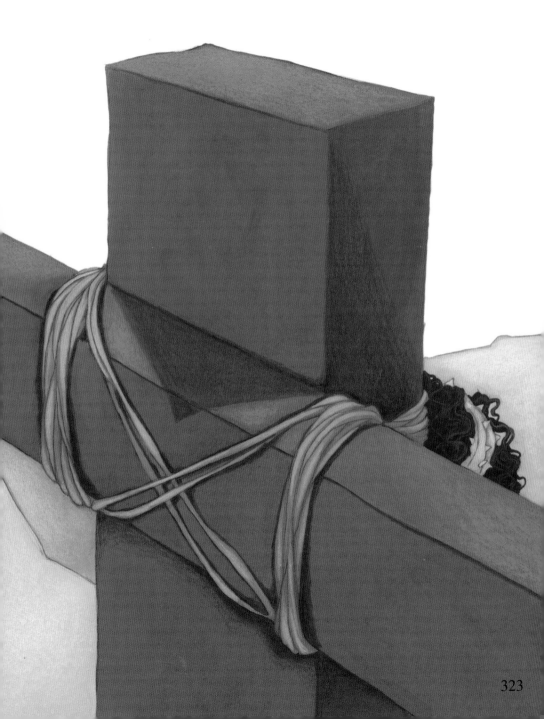

Jesus' friends
All wondered why
The Son of God
Would have to die.
They came and took
His body down
And sadly laid it
In the ground.
They sealed the tomb
And walked away.

There's never been
A sadder day.

JESUS IS ALIVE!
Matthew 28, John 20

Early Sunday morning
Before the light of day,
An angel came from heaven
And rolled the stone away.
Later on some women came
And looked into the tomb,
But Jesus wasn't in there—
It was an empty room!

The women told the others,
"He's gone! What will we do?"
So John and Peter ran to see
If what they said was true.
They saw the strips of cloth
That were lying on the ground,
But when they looked for Jesus,
He was nowhere to be found.

John and Peter went away,
But Mary stayed and cried.
Kneeling down beside the tomb
She took a look inside.
Imagine her surprise when
She looked inside the tomb,
And saw two angels dressed in white
Sitting in the room!

"I want to know where Jesus is,"
Mary sobbed and said.
But suddenly she heard a sound
That made her turn her head.
She thought it was the gardener
So she pleaded with the man,
"I want to know where Jesus is.
Please tell me if you can!"

But when the man said, "Mary!"
She lifted up her head.
This man was not the gardener—
"It's Jesus!" Mary said.
Jesus came alive again
That happy Easter day,
He bled and died
Then rose again
To take our sins away!

GOOD NEWS!

Luke 24, Acts 1–2

Jesus' friends were talking
Inside a darkened room,
For all of them had heard by now
About the empty tomb.
They told again the story
Of what the women said,
But how could Jesus be alive
When they had seen him dead?

And then two others
Came to tell
That they had seen him too.
They told how Jesus
Walked with them
And taught them
What was true.
"We did not know
That it was him,"
The two disciples said,
"Until he sat and
Ate with us,
And blessed and broke
The bread."

Jesus' friends were hiding.
Their hearts were filled with fear.
But suddenly they saw him—
Jesus had appeared!
Jesus said, "Don't be afraid,
Touch me and you'll see
That I am not a ghost at all—
Believe that it is me!"

341

Jesus told his friends to wait
There in Jerusalem.
He said his Holy Spirit
Would come and stay with them.
After this he went straight up
Before their very eyes
And disappeared
Among the clouds
High up in the sky.
As everyone was looking up,
They heard two angels say,
"Jesus will come back again
To be with you someday!"

The Holy Spirit came to them
Just as Jesus said.
He came with flames of fire
That landed on each head.
From that day on they told the world
The news about God's Son
And how he came to give new life
To each and every one!